DINOSAURS AND OTHER EXTINCT ANIMALS

(Original French title:
Dinosaures et Animaux Disparus)

by
Gabriel Beaufay

Translated from the French by
Albert V. Carozzi and Marguerite Carozzi

First English language edition published in 1987 by
Barron's Educational Series, Inc.

© 1986 Hachette S.A., 79, boulevard Saint-Germain, 75006 Paris

The title of the French edition is *Dinosaures et Animaux Disparus*.

International Standard Book No. 0-8120-3836-3

789 9687 987654321

New York • London • Toronto • Sydney

PRINTED IN FRANCE

Contents

Certain extinct animals and plants have left valuable remains preserved in rocks: fossils. This is the skeleton of an ancestor of birds, Archaeopteryx.

The Advent of Life

The planet earth was formed about 4.6 billion years ago (that is, 46 million centuries ago), a span of time that defies the imagination when compared with the relatively short duration of human life. This past is divided into five eras of decreasing duration: a very long one (4 billion years) called the Precambrian, followed by the Paleozoic, Mesozoic, Tertiary (Cenozoic) and Quaternary. We live in the Quaternary.

The first forms of life appeared during the Precambrian in the primitive ocean.

What is life? Where does it come from? In which form did it first appear? In the past, these questions gave rise to numerous philosophical and scientific theories. Today we have a more precise idea of the way things happened owing particularly to recent discoveries in biology and chemistry. Indeed, some scientists succeeded in reconstructing in the laboratory the natural conditions that existed on the surface of the globe more than 3 billion years ago. They artificially obtained the "particles" of the chemical chain that led to the appearance of the most primitive living beings.

The First Traces

The first living beings that generated in the oceans were said to be part of a "primitive soup." They were indeed extremely simple beings, no more than mere droplets of living matter. But in a relatively short time these droplets aggregated to become single-celled organisms, in particular bacteria. The struggle for life had started.

Other species appeared in the oceans: algae, jellyfish, corals, and mollusks. These organisms left remains: the oldest known fossils. As mentioned earlier, a fossil represents the skeleton, the shell, or any other part of the body of an

Volcanic eruptions, lightning, diluvial rains: Earth was not very hospitable some 4 billion years ago. Nevertheless, life was already beginning to appear in the oceans.

animal (or of a plant) that disappeared a long time ago and was preserved. Indeed, these remains were transformed: they are "petrified." At times, only imprints are found in rocks. The study of fossils is *paleontology*. This study allows us to reconstruct the major trends of life from the beginning to the present.

An Increasingly Richer Fauna

At the beginning of the Paleozoic, some 570 million years ago, all kinds of animals lived attached to the seafloor. These were sponges, brachiopods (with a shell resembling that of mollusks), and crinoids. Also called "sea lilies," crinoids are echinoderms (relatives of sea urchins and starfish) that look like flowers.

Orthoceras are extremely spectacular. Like our present day squid and octopus they are *cephalopods,* a name given to mollusks with a foot (*podos* in Greek), formed of tentacles and attached to the head (*kephal*). Orthoceras have a

In the oceans at the beginning of the Paleozoic an Orthoceras swims close to plantlike crinoids. The other organisms are reef-building corals.

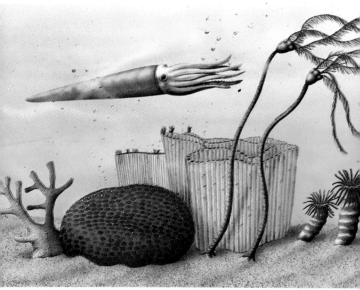

Vertebrates and Invertebrates

A crab has a very hard carapace, the snail has a shell. An antelope, an elephant, and a human being move on legs supported by bones. In other words, all these creatures have a skeleton.

But there are different kinds of skeletons. A crab, a snail, or a June bug has an external skeleton. By contrast, fish, amphibians, reptiles, birds, and mammals have an internal skeleton, characterized by an arrangement of bones forming the spinal, or vertebral, column. Animals with internal skeletons are called vertebrates *in contrast to* invertebrates, *such as mollusks, crustaceans, and insects.*

conical shell up to 4 meters (14 feet) long, often brilliantly colored, that remains horizontal in water. Orthoceras were fierce predators, hunting trilobites, for instance.

Trilobites are the most characteristic *arthropods* (or articulated and armored animals) of the Paleozoic seas. They resemble sowbugs. The name trilobite was given to them because their body is divided both longitudinally and transversally into three lobes. They crawled on the seafloor (their fossil trails were found!), but they also swam. Some of them certainly rolled up into a ball.

Eurypterids, also called "sea scorpions" although not true scorpions, were arthropods as long as 3 meters (10 feet). Eurypterids and trilobites have disappeared, but other strange arthropods from the Paleozoic seas still exist—horseshoe crabs with their characteristically rounded "shield." It is noteworthy that the larva of horseshoe crabs resembles a trilobite.

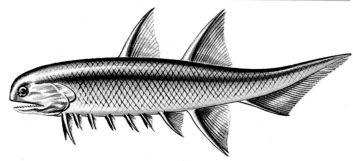

This armored fish, Climatius, somewhat resembles a shark. It has less armor than some other early fish.

Among the many invertebrates of the Paleozoic seas, the strangest are perhaps nautilids, goniatites, and graptolites. Nautilids, and horseshoe crabs, are both "living fossils." Nautilids, cephalopods with a spiral and pearly shell, still live in tropical seas. Goniatites are also cephalopods with a spiral shell, but they became extinct at the end of the Paleozoic.

Graptolites are small marine animals of the Paleozoic, most often floating (that is, *pelagic*). They formed colonies with cups gathered along an axis. Fossils of graptolites have been found in the black slates of Brittany and Calvados (in northwestern France).

The First Fishes

We do not know exactly when the first vertebrates appeared.

Nevertheless, some 500 million years ago they were already abundant.

The oldest vertebrates looked like fish. However, they were not true fish. They were Agnatha, meaning "jawless." They are represented today by

lampreys. In the Paleozoic, their head was usually protected by a bony shield. They lived close to the bottom of the sea and also in the bottom of freshwater lakes, extracting their food from mud. Some of them had three eyes! Whereas some were the ancestors of lampreys, others are the ancestors of fish.

Agnatha spread to freshwater lakes, and it was there that fish with bony jaws first appeared. Soon, these early fish were divided into several groups.

Acanthodians, such as Climatius, had bony spines at the front edge of their fins. They chased Agnatha.

Placoderms were even more impressive. They are the armored fish: the thorax was protected by a bony shield. Like *Dinichthys,* some were 12 meters (40 feet) long. After they entered the seas, they competed for a long time against the orthoceratids. Some of these placoderms lost their bony plates: thus began the cartilaginous fish, such as sharks and rays. The first shark, *Cladoselache,* had large rigid fins.

Dinichthys (the "terrible fish") well deserved its name. This armored fish had impressive teeth and was about 6 meters (20 feet) long. It was certainly the most feared predator of its time.

Toward Dry Land

Meanwhile, the conquest of dry land by living beings started. Plants were the first to do so.

At first living in the sea, algae started to invade fresh-water environments. Then they tried to live on the shore. In order to do that, they needed an impermeable covering.

Graptolites were floating colonial organisms. Each individual lived in a cup. These cups were arranged along an axis.

They also needed to be able to stand upright on the shore, and finally to extract water from the soil. A vascular system with thick walls allowed the plant to nourish itself and to be upright. Thus the first terrestrial plants appeared 400 million years ago. They consisted of a mere stem without a root or leaf.

Just as animals had done, plants multiplied and diversified. During the Carboniferous—the penultimate period of the Paleozoic—continents consisted of immense swamps and tropical forests. *Carboniferous* means coalbearing. Indeed, our coal was formed during that epoch. How? From the gradual decay within the soil of debris of plants forming these forests; hence these forests were called *coal-forming forests.*

These plants were gigantic tree ferns, horsetail, and lepidodendrons 45 meters (150 feet) high with numerous leaves. Horsetails are common in meadows, but present-day species are much smaller; they are called "horsetail" because of their bushy aspect. During the Carboniferous they reached a height of 30 meters (100 feet).

The invasion of the continents by plants had countless consequences.

The coal-forming forest was a landscape entirely unknown today. An intense animal life teemed in a humid and stifling atmosphere. Fossilization of these plants produced coal.

Why Plants First?

Most plants contain a green coloring matter, chlorophyll. It enables the plant to use solar energy (sunlight) to produce, from water and carbon dioxide in the air, the foodstuffs (sugars) that the plant needs to live. This process is called *photosynthesis.*

During this process, plants not only absorb carbon dioxide but in exchange they also release oxygen, the indispensable element for respiration in most living beings. Before the appearance of green plants, the atmosphere was devoid of oxygen. It consisted essentially of methane, ammonia, hydrogen, and water

11

Cycad and Ginkgo

Living fossils exist among both animals and plants. Such is the case of cycads. The stubby trunk carries a crown of large green leaves. They were abundant during the Mesozoic Era, but today they are restricted to tropical regions. The ginkgo, another living fossil, originated in China. Its fan-shaped leaves, which turn a beautiful golden yellow in the fall, earned its nickname "money tree."

Ginkgo leaf

Cycad

Giant dragonflies flew through the forests of the Carboniferous. In the same epoch, cockroaches reached a length of 20 centimeters (8 inches).

vapor. Furthermore, harmful ultraviolet radiation kept living organisms under water.

As soon as photosynthesis began to operate, oxygen spread into the atmosphere. A portion of the oxygen was transformed into ozone by ultraviolet radiation, thus creating a screen that this radiation could no longer cross. This allowed living beings to invade the air environment, which at the same time became "breathable." Indeed, the ability to leave the water was soon also going to affect some animals.

Animals Follow

About 350 million years ago, dry seasons, abundant rains, and droughts alternated. During a dry season, the streams and lakes emptied, leaving only small ponds in which fish could barely survive because

hey could not find enough oxygen. It is known that by means of their gills, fish use oxygen dissolved in water. Some fish developed a kind of lung, and started to breathe air.

Furthermore, after a pond dried up, some of these fish succeeded in crawling to another pond still containing water. Gradually, their fins changed into limbs. These fish are called crossopterygians. One of them survives today: it is the most famous living fossil, the coelacanth, discovered as late as 1938 in the Indian Ocean.

Fish gradually evolved into amphibians that were perfectly capable of walking on dry land. The oldest of these amphibians was *Ichthyostega*,

One of these three eusthenopterons, *fish of the Devonian, drags itself onto the shore of the pond. Another captures a fish. Eusthenopterons succeeded in leaving the water. Amphibians are their descendants.*

whose fossil remains were found in Greenland. Some of these early amphibians were bulky and somewhat resembled large salamanders. However, others became as slim as eels. All breathed air through their lungs. However, they had to return to water to lay their eggs.

These amphibians fed on fish, insects, or smaller amphibians. These animals were perfectly at home in the coal-forming forest described above. They had successfully left the water, one of the major events in the history of life. Many other bizarre species lived in the moist atmosphere of that forest: scorpions, spiders, cockroaches, sap-sucking insects, and centipedes 2 meters (7 feet) long. Giant dragonflies with a wing span of 75 centimeters (30 inches) buzzed in the air.

Truly Terrestrial: The Reptiles

Some amphibians continued to evolve. Some became the frogs and toads that we know today. Others started to lay eggs on the ground rather than in water. These eggs were protected by a shell and were less likely to be eaten by predators. On the ground, eggs could easily be hidden. Thus these species could survive when the climate of the earth became more arid and when the grea

Mastodonsaurus was a stubby amphibian with a large head. Its remains were discovered in Alsace (in northeastern France) and in Germany.

Eryops was also a stubby amphibian, resembling an enormous salamander.

Diadectes was a particularly important amphibian with respect to evolution. Aspects of its appearance foreshadow the reptiles. Notice its powerful legs, which served to walk away from water.

swamps dried up. These amphibians became the first reptiles, animals that were completely free from the aquatic environment.

The first reptiles resembled large lizards. Some were very important; they are called mammallike reptiles because they are distant ancestors of mammals. All were carnivorous animals that ate insects or mollusks. The largest among them also ate the smaller ones.

One of the most remarkable of these reptiles was Dimetrodon. It was 3 meters (10 feet) long and carried on its back a kind of crest supported by long bony spines. What was the use of this crest? It was formerly believed that the animal used it as a sail when swimming in a lake. Probably not. The crest may have served instead to regulate the temperature of the animal. Indeed such a crest may have helped to either heat or cool the body.

Mammallike reptiles became very abundant. Little by little, they ceased to crawl and their legs straightened and raised the body farther off the ground. They acquired the characteristics of mammals: their scales were replaced by hair and mammary glands.

Dimetrodon (illustrated below) is the most famous among primitive reptiles. It had teeth not only in its jaw but also on its palate.

Lycaenops. *Some 200 million years old, it was already a mammallike reptile. Quite straight on its legs, it was 1 meter (3 feet) long.*

appeared. Mammals emerged at the beginning of the Meso-zoic, but for a long time they played a minor role in the fauna. Other animals came to the forefront—first, the dinosaurs.

The Reign of Giants

The Mesozoic was above all the age of large reptiles. All natural environments were invaded by these extraordinary and often gigantic animals, whose names end in "saur" (from the Greek sauro, *meaning lizard): brontosaurs, gigantosaurs, and other dinosaurs; pterosaurs, ichthyosaurs, plesiosaurs, and many more. Some species with less fantastic looks were of great importance because a few evolved into mammals (as mentioned above) and others into birds. Let us not forget marine invertebrates; during the Mesozoic, ammonites and the astonishing rudists diversified in the seas.*

The Mesozoic Era is divided into three periods: the Triassic, the Jurassic, and the Cretaceous. During the Triassic, ammonites appeared and thrived until the end of the Mesozoic. They were cephalopod mollusks with a spiral shell. The shell varied greatly from one species to the other. Some displayed transverse ribs, others, nodes.

Rudists were also mollusks, but they were part of the lamellibranchs or bivalves—or, in other words, mollusks with two valves, such as mussels and oysters.

The thick shell of rudists was provided with a strongly toothed hinge. The rudists' main characteristic was their adaptation to reef life. Indeed, the banks they formed constituted true reefs comparable to the coral reefs in present-day seas. During the Mesozoic, rudists and corals were often associated in the same reefs.

Some rudists were attached to the bottom of the sea by the left valve of the shell; in these species the two valves were of almost equal size. Other rudists were attached by the right valve. This valve sometimes had the shape of an ice-cream cone, whereas the left one looked like a lid.

Ammonites, *mollusks that appeared about 200 million years ago, included gigantic species.*

This impressive reef *(below) consists of several species of rudists. These strange mollusks became extinct at the end of the Mesozoic Era.*

The Appearance of the Dinosaurs

Dinosaurs first appeared in the Triassic. In spite of their name—dinosaur means "terrible lizard"—they were in the beginning relatively small. Small dinosaurs occurred even in the middle of th Mesozoic Era, such as *Comp sognathus,* whose length di not exceed 60 centimeters (2 inches).

Simultaneously, the hour o the giants had come. Diversifi cation of their shapes mad some stubby and others elon gated. *Plateosaurus,* fo

Near a primitive turtle, a Rhynchosaurus seems to watch over a swamp with few primitive dinosaurs. Rhynchosaurus must have fed on hard-shelled fruit, a suggested by a beaklike structure at the end of its snout.

nstance, was a long-necked nd small-headed vegetarian, ertainly capable of standing pright on two legs from time o time.

Dinosaurs are classified ccording to the structure of heir pelvis. Some have a lizrd-type pelvis, hence their ame *saurischia;* others have a bird-type pelvis, hence their name *ornithischia.* The best known dinosaurs belong to the saurischia, such as *Diplodocus,* a probable descendant of *Plateosaurus.* They were thick-bodied quadrupeds with a small head at the end of a long neck and with a rather long tail. Their legs were truly

pillars. The whole length of *Diplodocus* reached 25 meters (80 feet).

Other dinosaurs of the same group were even larger, including Gigantosaurus ("giant lizard") and Brachiosaurus. They reached sizes up to 40 meters (130 feet). All the records appear broken by *Supersaurus,* recently discovered in Colorado, which would have reached 50 meters (160 feet). However, it is known only by a few bones.

Thus, dinosaurs of this type exceeded in length any recent large cetaceans; the most important of them, the blue whale, reaches only 30 meters (100 feet). However, the large dinosaurs, because of their neck and their tail, had a smaller body mass and hence a lighter weight, namely about 40 to 60 tons versus 150 tons for the blue whale.

Harmless Vegetarians...

Diplodocus and its relatives were herbivores. They were, after all, only tranquil giants. In general, they are illustrated splashing in the water o swamps or ponds. But wer they really amphibious? Sci entists are not sure. Som paleontologists think that the lived on dry ground.

Indeed, their morphology i more like that of terrestrial ani mals. Furthermore, the tail di not touch the ground. Foot prints of these dinosaurs wer found unaccompanied by an traces of a tail. They coul have led a life similar to that o present-day giraffes. Lik them, they would have fed o tall trees and perhaps lived i rather large groups.

...And Fearsome Carnivores

Other dinosaurs with a lizard type pelvis were, on the con trary, bipeds. They stood o their hindlegs somewhat lik kangaroos. They were gener ally carnivores. *Struthiomi mus* resembled an ostrich. I was toothless but certainly ha a horned beak. It must hav preyed on the eggs of othe dinosaurs.

Tyrannosaurus is the mos famous. It was a powerful ca

Brachiosaurus *shown in water (right). Are such reconstructions correct Experts still argue about the living conditions of the great dinosaurs.*

In the forefront, a biped running dinosaur. In the background, two Stegosaurus (left), an Iguanodon (center), and two Brachiosaurus (right). It is known today that some dinosaurs lived in colonies: the young remained for a certain time in the nest, where they were fed by their parents. Dinosaur eggs were discovered on Mt. Sainte-Victoire, in Provence (in southeastern France).

Fossils from Antarctica

Fossils of amphibians and mammallike reptiles were discovered in the center of the Antarctic continent. The same genera were also found in South Africa and in Australia. Geologists see in this an additional proof in favor of the theory that all these land masses formed a single continent during the Paleozoic. This extensive continent broke up into parts that drifted over the heavier and more stable oceanic substratum. This process is called continental drift.

nivore with a skull 1.4 meters (4.5 feet) long and impressive teeth. Most certainly, it killed its prey with the help of its hind legs. It used its small forelegs and its teeth only to tear apart the dead victims. Relatives of *Tyrannosaurus* had a sickle-shaped nail at the end of the hindthumb with which they could disembowel their prey.

Well-Protected Species

Dinosaurs with a birdlike pelvis, the Ornithischians, were extremely diversified. Some of them were vegetarian bipeds. The best known is *Iguanodon*, about 10 meters (30 feet) long. The thumb of its forelegs is truly a spur. It probably used it to tear off the branches it ate.

A related genus, *Trachodon* had a beak similar to that of a duck but provided with about 2000 small teeth. It has been possible to examine its skin, perfectly preserved since the Mesozoic, a rare occurrence among dinosaurs. Belonging to the same group were *Hypsilophodon,* probably capable of climbing trees, and *Hadrosaurus,* adorned with a bony crest on its head.

Other ornithischians had bulky shapes. Thus, *Stegosaurus,* 6 to 8 meters (20 to 27 feet) long, was a large quadruped with a back armed with rows of triangular plates on which its enemies broke their teeth. Furthermore, its tail had long spikes. *Ankylosaurus,* with its protective armor of bony plates, was not handicapped. Like an armadillo, its bony plates made it invincible. This protection was enhanced on the sides by long sharp spikes and at the end of the tail by a kind of club. *Ankylosaurus'* only weakness was the possibility of being turned on its back by a predator.

"Bulldozers"

There was yet another lineage of dinosaurs with a birdlike pelvis altogether different. *Protoceratops* was 2 meters (7 feet) and had a parrotlike beak and a bony shield to protect its neck. Eggs of this dinosaur still

Tyrannosaurus often inspires novelists and movie producers. This terrifying superpredator has no equivalent in the present-day fauna. It was 10 meters (30 feet) long and 2.5 meters (8 feet) high, and weighed about 7 tons.

containing skeletons of embryos were found in the Gobi Desert. The same group also included its giants, in particular *Triceratops*. This bulky dinosaur was the size of a rhinoceros and also somewhat resembled it. Its neck was also protected by a collar of bony plates. Furthermore, as indicated by its name, it carried three horns, a short one above the snout and two long ones above the orbits. A related genus, *Styracosaurus,* had a collarlike shield armed with spikes.

Scientists assume that these dinosaurs were attacked by the terrible *Tyrannosaurus,* which nevertheless had a tough time killing them. Indeed, *Triceratops* were like living tanks, probably capable of running 50 kilometers (30 miles) per hour. Whenever *Tyrannosaurus* appeared on the horizon, like a gigantic kangaroo sitting on a tripod consisting of its hindlegs and tail, *Triceratops* could conceivably charge it like a bulldozer and try to overturn it.

All this may seem like fiction...but it is not necessarily. Detailed study of the skeletons of vanished animals allows us to reconstruct their living habits with some certainty. Thus it is possible to have an idea of the struggle for life on the surface of the globe in these remote times—not only on land, but also in the air.

Like an Aztec God

Let us imagine a Mesozoic landscape—for instance, a wooded plain somewhat similar to the present-day savanna of East Africa. A few brontosaurs quietly graze. Suddenly an extraordinary animal with membranous wings similar to those of a bat appears in the sky. It glides weightlessly, reacting to the slightest breeze. It operates with great skill, inspecting with large eyes the surface of a pond. Suddenly, it dives toward the water and climbs back up with a fish in its beak.

This animal was a flying reptile or *Pterosaurus* ("winged lizard"). Indeed, a group of Mesozoic reptiles conquered the air. They had long membranous wings supported by very enlongated fourth finger of the "hand."

The size of pterosaurs varied

Iguanodon tearing off branches. Numerous skeletons of Iguanodon were found in various places. These dinosaurs are among the best known by paleontologists.

Parasaurolophus had a crest on its head reaching 1.50 meters (5 feet)! What was its use? Air supply for diving, ornaments for courtship displays, echo chamber? Nobody knows.

greatly. Some were as small as sparrows, whereas others were as large as eagles. *Pteranodon* had a wingspan of 8 meters (26 feet). This nightmarish creature had a long toothless beak that was counterbalanced by a bony crest extending behind its skull.

For a long time, it was considered the largest flying reptile until an even larger pterosaur was discovered in Texas. The size of its bones indicated that it might have reached 15.5 meters (51 feet). It was called *Quetzalcoatlus* in honor of the Aztec god Quetzalcoatl, whose emblem was a flying snake.

Another extraordinary fact about reptiles: some pterosaurs were covered with hair. (Hair is considered a characteristic of mammals.)

Wind Tunnel Tests

Where did these extraordinary flying reptiles live? Most of them must have dwelled on sea cliffs where they could cling to rocks as swifts do. In order to take off, again as do swifts, they simply let themselves drop. Others certainly perched in trees, at least in places where they did not run any risk of tearing their wings.

Still others landed on the ground. But how could they take off? Simply by stretching their wings, provided that winds were sufficiently strong to carry them away like feathers. It is important to stress that the bones of these reptiles were filled with air, like those of birds, which made them very light.

If we are so well informed

bout their behavior, it is because investigators had the clever idea to construct scale models and test them in wind tunnels.

Most of these animals probably caught fish by diving at the surface of lakes or of the sea. Others were unquestionably scavengers. For instance, whenever gigantic *Quetzalcoatlus*, gliding in the sky, noticed the corpse of a dino-saur, they dropped onto the corpse and devoured it in a confusing mess of beaks, necks, and wings! An incredible show that we can only imagine, not having been able to see it.

Shapes of Dolphins

After having invaded dry land and the sky, reptiles took to the

riceratops resembled a rhinoceros. In many respects dinosaurs played during the Mesozoic Era the same ecologic role as present-day large mammals that live, for instance, in the African savannas.

sea. Three main groups flourished there: ichthyosaurs, plesiosaurs, and mosasaurs. It is noteworthy that these three types of marine reptiles were not at all constructed in the same way. This shows that when evolution faces the same problems, it can lead to different solutions.

Imagine a dolphin, not with two but with four flippers; you would get an approximate picture of an *Ichthyosaurus* ("sea serpent"). Ichthyosaurs, often longer than 10 meters (30 feet), had a very hydrodynamic shape. Like cetaceans, they had a dorsal fin devoid of a skeleton. They had a long snout with numerous teeth. By means of their large eyes, they hunted fish near the surface of the water.

The shape of ichthyosaurs not only resembles that of dolphins but also resembles the equally hydrodynamic shape of sharks and tunas. This is an example of convergence, a principle according to which several species leading the same kind of life may look alike.

The Stuttgart Museum (in West Germany) displays the skeleton of a female ichthyosaur giving birth. Indeed, without limbs, ichthyosaurs could not move on solid ground and hence never left the aquatic environment. They were necessarily viviparous, whereas the great majority of reptiles lay eggs.

Ichthyosaurs, plesiosaurs and mosasaurs were the major marine reptiles of the Mesozoic Era. They were not alone. During their wandering through the immense oceans they might have encountered monstrous fishtailed crocodiles, huge turtles, and many other reptiles.

On dry land many other strange reptiles also existed. All these fabulous animals, dinosaurs, marine reptiles, and flying reptiles became extinct at the end of the Mesozoic Era. Some of them had obviously disappeared earlier but had been replaced by others. Final extinction occured at the end of the Cretaceous. Why?

Scenarios for a Catastrophe

A huge meteorite sped toward the earth. At 1,500,000 kilometers (about 1,000,000 miles)

A Stegosaurus being attacked by a carnivorous dinosaur.

per hour, it penetrated the atmosphere of our planet and then crashed with a terrible shock. The impact of the meteorite generated a cloud of dust that spread all around the globe. This dust prevented solar radiation from reaching the earth, which was plunged into darkness. Vegetation dwindled, and dinosaurs died for lack of food.

This is one of several possible scenarios for the extinction of Mesozoic reptiles. This hypothesis has been very popular during recent years. Indeed, iridium, a little known metal, was discovered in several locations in layers of rocks dating back to the end of the Mesozoic. Since iridium occurs mainly in meteorites, some scientists theorized that a large meteorite had hit the earth at that particular time.

Hence, death would have come to dinosaurs from the sky. This is not the first time this idea has been suggested. Indeed, the deadly effects of a possible and relatively close supernova were considered. A supernova is a star that ends its life in an explosion. Suddenly, its luminosity becomes extraordinary. According to astronomers, a supernova certainly exploded at the end of the Cretaceous. Its explosion would have generated a tremendous amount of X-rays

and cosmic rays that dealt a death blow to the dinosaurs.

Such hypotheses are certainly attractive. However, how can one explain that this "death from the sky" hit the dinosaurs but spared the rela

Pterodactyls flying over Stegosaurus. *Flying reptiles have always excited the human imagination: for instance,* The Lost World, *the famous novel by Arthur Conan Doyle.*

ively small but already very numerous mammals?

Other hypotheses appear similarly tenuous. We know that when its members become very large, an evolu- tionary lineage often disap- pears. But small dinosaurs became extinct at the same time as the large ones. Then was a malfunctioning of the endocrine glands responsible?

Ichthyosaurs, with their hydrodynamic shape, swam at great speed. They did not lay eggs; they were viviparous, the females giving birth to well-formed young.

Poisoning, Epidemics, Parasites?

Dinosaurs may have been poisoned by toxic plants. Indeed, during the Cretaceous, flowering plants spread over the earth. They may contain alkaloids, substances harmful for animals that eat them. They were dangerous for reptiles in particular because reptiles are less sensitive to their unpleasant taste than mammals.

Devouring enormous quantities of plants, reptiles ran high risks of becoming poisined even though they have taste buds, which are located beneath the tongue. Furthermore, they have a powerful defense mechanism consisting of enzymes that act against vegetable poisons. In any case the poisoning theory would explain the extinction of neither carnivorous dinosaurs nor marine reptiles.

Is it then necessary to assume an epidemic on a planetary scale, fatal parasites, or the actions of the first mammals? Or perhaps droughts or floods? Or toxic gases? Or is it necessary to give up and admit our ignorance?

The most reasonable hypothesis is the one that suggests a large-scale climatic event. At the end of the Mesozoic a general retreat of the seas in fact took place, what geologists call a marine regression. Continents emerged and increased in size. It is known that the farther an area is from the sea the more severe is its climate. Such a climate, with harsh winters, may have killed the dinosaurs. Other reptiles may have survived these bad seasons by hibernating in burrows or hiding places. Thus, they may have survived until today.

But this, too, is only a hypothesis.

The Takeover

At the end of the Mesozoic, dinosaurs, pterosaurs, and marine reptiles became extinct. Turtles, snakes, crocodiles, and lizards survived. Two other lines were going to have an extraordinary fate.

Let us recall the mammallike reptiles. Starting in the Trias-

Group of plesiosaurs (together with an ichthyosaur). Remains of these reptiles were found at Cap de la Hève near Le Havre, a harbor in northwestern France.

Large marine lizards, mosasaurs also resembled crocodiles. Perhaps they swam upstream to give birth to their young in water. Underneath the mosasaur swims a Geosaurus.

sic, their descendants appeared, the first mammals. These were modest-looking animals. During all of the Mesozoic Era, they led very discrete lives—under the feet of the dinosaurs, we might say. These animals, which were probably nocturnal, looked like shrews. They were waiting for their turn. During the Cretaceous they started to diversify.

At the same time, another lineage of reptiles produced birds. This lineage seems to have originated among dinosaurs, specifically dinosaurs with birdlike pelvic bones. Some experts have found so many resemblances between these dinosaurs and birds that they named the latter "feather-clad reptiles." However, not everybody agrees with this interpretation.

A Venerable Ancestor

During the Jurassic the first bird appeared, *Archaeopteryx*, still half-reptile. It was as large as a pigeon and was covered with feathers. However, its beak still had teeth and its tail was that of a reptile with some twenty vertebrae.

Its wings were well formed, with claws that could probably hold on to branches. It is noteworthy that a bird actually exists today in the Amazon

Archaeopteryx must have looked colors of its feathers are not known.

basin whose young also ha claws on its wings. It is th hoatzin, a remote relative o the cuckoo.

Could *Archaeopteryx* reall fly, or was it content to glic from tree to tree? We canno tell. According to a recer hypothesis, the forelimbs the ancestors of *Archeoptery* which were spread out whi running, became traps fe insects. These natural "fl

ike this. However, the precise

"traps" later changed into wings. At any rate, *Archeopteryx* is an ideal link between reptiles and birds.

Its direct descendants appeared during the Cretaceous, some 130 million years ago. One, *Hesperornis,* a large aquatic bird, 1 meter (3 feet) long, had rudimentary wings and must have resembled our present diver. It still possessed teeth. It must have constantly lived on high seas and came to shore only to reproduce. Ichthyornis, dating also from the Cretaceous, resembled a gull.

At the end of the Mesozoic, birds had diversified and included types that looked like flamingos, pelicans, kingfishers, and woodpeckers. Mammals were also ready to begin their reign.

The Era of Mammals

When the Tertiary Era began, the earth seemed devoid of large animals. Giant reptiles were gone, there were few birds, and mammals were small. But evolution was continuing. Changes occurred, mostly in mammals, which continuously diversifed with some of them increasing in size. They were also to undergo a true radiation ("explosion") in all directions, especially with respect to horns, antlers, and tusks.

Starting in the Eocene (about 50 million years ago), hoofed mammals (*ungulates*) diversified. Ungulates are the largest terrestrial mammals, represented today by cattle, deer, giraffes, pigs, elephants, and horses.

At the beginning of the Tertiary, the ancestors of horses were about the size of a fox. Their descendants gradually increased in size to reach that of the present-day horse. This evolution occurred in North America. Horses then migrated to Europe across Asia, and strangely enough disappeared from North America. They were reintroduced by Spanish conquerors after the discovery of the New World by Christopher Columbus.

In South America lived closely related animals—litopterna. One of them, *Macrauchenia,* presents difficult problems to paleontologists. According to the structure of its skull, it must have had a small trunk. But it also had a long neck and thin legs. However, according to some

The strange Macrauchenia, a primitive ungulate, is generally represented with a trunk. But it is not certain that it really carried such a proboscis.

experts, long necks and thin legs are incompatible with a trunk. Did *Macrauchenia* live in steppes or in marshes? Nobody knows the answer to this question, either.

Macrauchenia lived together with *Toxodon*, another strange hoofed mammal. This bulky animal, large as a rhinoceros, with an arched back, was probably a bur

South American landscape during the Pliocene. *Toxodons in the foreground, Macrauchenias in the pond. In the background Thylacosmilus (saber-toothed marsupials) are hunting litopterna, which resemble horses.*

ower. It must have dug impressive holes. The true rhinoceros evolved during the Tertiary. Some of them were remarkable, such as *Baluchitherium*, or "beast of Balu-

chistan" (therium from the Greek *therion*, "wild beast"), which measured more than 5 meters (17 feet) at the *withers* (highest part of the base of the neck of a hoofed mammal). In other words, its withers were at the same height as the horns of a present-day giraffe. It was the largest land mammal of all time.

Another unusual rhinoceros was *Elasmotherium*. It carried an enormous horn on its forehead. It was also a gigantic beast, although smaller than *Baluchitherium*.

Trunk and Tusks: Mastodons

Proboscidians, the order that at present includes elephants, appeared in Egypt during the Eocene, with *Moeritherium* reaching only 60 centimeters (24 inches) at the withers. It must have resembled a tapir.

Later, proboscidians increased in size. The snout became a trunk and the incisors, tusks. Some of them had tusks on both jaws. These mastodon reached an enormous size, and their name has became a popular expression for something huge. Several types of mastodons existed with a *mandible* (bone of the lower jaw) shaped as a shovel, a pick, or even a beak.

A somewhat different proboscidian was *Dinotherium* with a mandible that carried backward-curving tusks. Unquestionably the animal used them to dig. *Dinotherium* survived until the Quaternary in Western Africa and was contemporary of the first human beings.

What Is a Marsupial?

Marsupials represent a particular group of mammals. Their young are born partially formed and complete their growth in a ventral pouch of the female. Kangaroos are the best known marsupials. All marsupials, with the exception of the opossum of Virginia, live in Australia and South America.

Dinotherium *was known in East Africa by Australopithecus, our ancestor, which appeared about 4 million years ago.*

Numerous but Often Threatened

There are many more strange hoofed mammals.

Dinoceras was more than 2 meters (7 feet) high at the withers. Its flat head was almost reptilian. Two long pointed tusks adorned its upper jaw and three pairs of horns its forehead.

Baluchitherium, *was one of the largest terrestrial mammals of all time. Its feet had only three toes.*

Moropus resembled a giraffe but had a shortened neck and a horselike head. A related form *Chalicotherium,* had longer forelegs than hindlegs. It was nicknamed "horse-gorilla," and it also survived quite late in Africa.

The incredible *Arsinoitherium* was 1.5 meters (5 feet) high at the withers and 3 meters (10 feet) long and carried four horns, with the frontal horns much more developed.

Paleotherium looked like a tapir; *Anoplotherium* was stubby with a long tail; and *Xiphodon* was as graceful as a gazelle. These three species lived where the city of Paris, France, is found. The French paleontologist Georges Cuvier

Gnathobelodon was a strange mastodon with a shovel-shaped lower mandible. Some mastodons lived in the Andes at elevations.

A Living Fossil: The Okapi

At the beginning of the twentieth century, a fossil mammal of the Tertiary was discovered in the African forest: the okapi. This relative of the giraffe is indeed very similar to the Helladotherium of the Miocene. It lives in the Ituri forest of Zaire. The okapi, truly a living fossil, survived in a refuge provided by the great African forest. It was considered a horse before its relationship with the giraffe was recognized.

*These **machairodus** look like gentle big cats. In fact, they were dangerous killing machines: their canines were 10 to 15 centimeters (**4 to 6 inches**) long.*

ound their fossil remains at e beginning of the nineenth century while investiating the rocks of the Montmartre hill.

These herbivores did not ad a peaceful life. Indeed, ey were prey to dangerous rnivores. The most impresve predators were the felines ats), whose upper canines ecame terrible saberlike teeth. Therefore they are called saber-toothed tigers, such as *Machairodus* and *Smilodon*.

Among Other "Families"

Strangely enough, some fossil marsupials also had saberlike canines. This is another example of convergence, as previ-

Smilodon, relative of Machairodus, is represented here in an aggressive attitude. In Europe, human ancestors did not know such beasts.

A formidable beak, legs adapted to running, but no wings: this is Diatryma, nicknamed "terror crane."

ously discussed. They wer obviously carnivores.

Marsupials also evolve during the Tertiary, and som of them reached an apprecia ble size. Such is the case c diprotodons from Australia which were as large and heav as a rhinoceros and becam extinct only recently.

By the way, giant forr existed in most groups c mammals, including th rodents, which are not ver large today. A giant roden such as *Megamys,* was in fa very imposing looking: thin about a coypu (yielding the f nutria) the size of a rhinocero

Cetaceans also evolved i the Tertiary, developing fro terrestrial mammals th earched for food in the sea. They gradually lost their legs and became completely aquatic animals. From them the whales and other aquatic giants were to evolve as we know them today.

Several lines of primates evolved: lemurs, monkeys, anthropoid apes, and finally the human lineage, which flourished in the Quaternary, our era.

Impressive Birds

We interrupted our discussion of birds when they began to diversify toward the end of the Mesozoic. In the Tertiary, the major groups of present-day birds existed. The most interesting event was the appearance of gigantic and impressive, but flightless, birds.

For instance, *Phororhacos* ran on the plains of Patagonia. Taller than a human being, it had an enormous head and beak that together reached over 65 centimeters (26 inches) in length. There is no doubt that this terrifying bird made life difficult for the mammals that shared its environment.

Diatryma, rather similar to *Phororhacos,* lived mainly in the Old World. Its fossil remains were found near Reims, France. Dark and filamentous feathers discovered in Colorado seem to belong to the same kind of bird. Therefore, *Diatryma* had relatives on the North American continent.

Another giant bird of the Tertiary lived in the area where Paris was later built. Therefore, it well deserves its Latin name *Gastornis parisensis.* Of large size, it had a big head and long powerful legs.

Eventually, all these large birds became extinct. However, some of the smaller species, found today in tropical forests, lived in Europe a few million years ago. For instance, the phosphorites of Quercy (in southwestern France), which are phosphatic concretions, contain the remains of the secretary bird. Today, this voracious snake hunter lives in Africa.

Deadly Sands

Tertiary fossils were often well preserved. Therefore, it is possible to reconstruct episodes, sometimes dramatic ones, of past wildlife.

Millions of bones were discovered, for instance, in sandy hills along a valley in Nebraska. These bones belong to three kinds of mammals: the previously mentioned *Moropus, Dinohyus,* which looked like a giant buffalo-sized pig, and *Diceratherium,* a small rhinoceros with two horns.

When these animals lived in the Miocene (about 20 million years ago), a large river ran through Nebraska. During the dry season, the valley changed into a sandy plain covered by shallow water. *Moropus, diceratherium,* and *Dinohyus* came to drink—and sank into quicksand.

Let us imagine the event. Thousands of small rhinoceroses pushed and shoved each other, grunting and stabbing with their horns. *Moropus* and the giant pigs tried to find a passage in their midst but soon became imprisoned in the swarming mass.

The first diceratheriums, realizing the danger, tried to stop, but others continued to push them and they were all trapped.

Millions of years later, the astounding accumulation of their skeletons was found. This discovery is comparable to that of the almost perfectly preserved remains of mammoths found in the frozen peats of Siberia. But this brings us to the Quaternary.

Syntethoceras *(about 7 million years ago) had a horn on its snout as did the legendary unicorn. This ruminant lived in North America.*

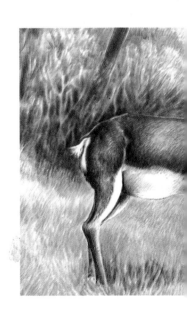

A Few "Birth Dates"

Approximate time of appearance of the direct ancestors of some present-day wild animals (figures in millions of years).

Scorpion	390	Hedgehog	20
Spider	345	Seal	20
Crocodile	190	Dolphin	15
Armadillo	60	Hippopotamus	10
White shark	50	Elephant	10
Cobra	50	Deer	7
Great horned owl	35	Fox	7
Albatross	30	Kangaroo	7
Marmoset	28	Chimpanzee	4
Panda	25	Lion	4
Swallow	25	Brown bear	1

Toward the Present Fauna

We live in the Quaternary. This period, still continuing, is in fact very short compared with earlier periods; it began only 4 million years ago. It is particularly important for the evolution of primates, which led to the human race. But during this period, astonishing and often large species of mammals and birds also lived: mammoths, woolly rhinoceroses, great cave bears, giant sloths, and moas. Our ancestors knew them and hunted them.

The imperial mammoth reigned over the wooded plains of North America. This colossal animal was more than 4 meters (14 feet) high at the withers and must have weighed 20 tons.

However, whenever one talks about mammoths in general, the Siberian mammoth is meant. This animal indeed lived in Siberia but also lived in Europe. Its natural habitat was the forest (not the tundra, as is commonly believed). This is certainly true because forest plants were found in the stomachs of mammoths, beautifully preserved in the frozen Siberian muds. Indeed, mammoths are found in mud but not in ice, as is often erroneously mentioned.

Painted on the walls of some caves in Europe by human beings, the Siberian mammoth was smaller than its American relative. It was no taller than 3 meters (10 feet) at the withers but two humps, one on the head and the other on the withers, gave it an impressive look. Its curved tusks pointed forward, and its woolly fleece had a reddish or yellowish sheen.

In Siberia, mammoth tusks were found in such great numbers that they led to a flourishing commerce—120,000 were sold in one century.

Well-Protected Against the Cold

During the Quaternary, the northern glaciers advanced and retreated several times. The fauna of Europe varied according to the rhythm of these four glaciations. The mammoth was not really suited for a cold climate, but it adapted to it thanks to a thick layer of fat for protection against the cold.

Another animal adapted very well to glacial climate, the woolly rhinoceros. It was as tall as the present-day rhinoceros and carried on its snout two horns, the frontal one reaching 1.5 meters (5 feet). It was covered by a thick black and reddish fleece.

Remains of the woolly rhinoceros were also discovered in the frozen muds of Siberia. These remains were mummified in ozokerite, a kind of nat-

Mammoths in the snow-covered taiga. Such a sight was familiar to early Europeans, for whom the mammoth was both a source of food and artistic inspiration.

In the past, fossil skulls *of the woolly rhinoceros were considered dragon heads and its horns the claws of giant birds.*

ural paraffin. Study of the contents of the stomachs revealed that this species fed mainly on conifer needles.

This animal also dwelled in Europe; a cave painting at La Colombière, close to Nantua (Ain, France), shows a woolly rhinoceros with its belly riddled with arrows.

Wild Oxen, Deer, and Large Carnivores

The auroch was impressive too. We know this wild ox we[ll] not only because prehistori[c] caves, in particular at Lascau[x] (in southern France), displa[y] splendid illustrations of thi[s] animal but also because it survived until historic times.

The auroch measured up to 2 meters (7 feet) at the withers. It had lyre-shaped horns. The male had a black coat, but the female's was reddish. One should not confuse the aurochs with the bison. The latter as well as elks (and moose), reindeer, and wild horses were hunted by our ancestors.

Megaceros is one of the most famous prehistoric mammals. It is the great deer of the bogs, in particular those of Ireland. It had gigantic webbed antlers that spanned up to 3.5 meters (12 feet). We know that it fell victim to these antlers: eventually it could not carry them any longer because they were too heavy—and *Megaceros* became extinct.

Large carnivores that the early Europeans had to fight lived in caves. However, the cave lion, a large and very lithe feline with a slightly banded fur, does not deserve its name because, in fact, it lived instead in the steppes and the forests.

The great cave bear reached a height of 2.50 meters (8 feet) when upright. Its forelegs were very long so that its front body was raised; it must have had an arched appearance. Human beings used traps or nets to capture it, to get its meat, bone marrow, fur, claws, and teeth. But were humans always victorious in their fights with this dangerous animal?

Megaceros sinking into a bog. It is condemned to a long agony unless its splendid antlers can be used as support on solid ground.

59

In the Cave of the Ultima Esperanza

At the southern tip of South America, not very far from the Strait of Magellan, is the cave of the Ultima Esperanza (last hope). What was found there indeed inspired a last hope to rediscover a fantastic mammal that had survived from a rather remote past.

In 1895, a German sea captain ventured into this cave, which is as large as a cathedral. He found there a strange piece of leather, 1.50 meters (5 feet) long and 70 centimeters (28 inches) wide, covered with reddish hair and backed by small bones.

In this cave, he discovered furthermore a human skeleton, enormous excrements, and a large pile of fodder. Moreover, small stone walls indicated that humans had wanted to close off the entrance to the cave.

All that remained to be done was to reconstruct what might have happened in the cave of the Ultima Esperanza. The piece of skin belonged to a giant ground sloth. Modern species of sloths, the slow-moving edentate mammals of South America, are the size of a cat. However, in the past, some like Mylodon were as tall as an ox and others, like Megatherium, as tall as an elephant.

Of course, they were unable to climb trees; they merely stood in order to eat the leaves. Humans sometimes chased the animal to a cave and shut it in to eat it some day. This is what happened at the Ultima Esperanza cave.

The remains of the giant sloth were so fresh that an immense hope was kindled: perhaps these huge mammals are still alive? Around 1900, the newspaper headlines were as big as those about the discovery of the okapi. Expeditions were undertaken to discover the giant sloths, but none were found.

It resembles both the bear and the kangaroo. *This Megatherium, a giant sloth, eats leaves that it grabs with its long tongue. The Paris Museum owns a beautiful skeleton of this animal.*

Other Lost Species

Gigantic armadillos, called glyptodons, reached 4 meters (14 feet) in length. They were covered by a rigid domed carapace; their head was covered by a kind of helmet. The tail sometimes terminated in a spiky club. In short, the description makes us immediately think about dinosaurs. But the resemblance stops there.

Indians also knew them. They painted them on cave walls and used their carapaces as shelters. It is now established that none of these species survived.

The Largest Bird of All Time

We are not quite finished with the giants of the Quaternary. In order to discover others, we must turn to birds.

Madagascar was the home of huge birds, the *Aepyornis.* Imagine heavy ostriches, 3 meters (10 feet) high and weighing more than 400 kilograms. It seems unnecessary to say that they could not fly. Their eggs were 32 centimeters (12 inches) long and 22 centimeters (8 inches) wide. Each could have contained 140 chicken eggs! *Aepyornis* survived until the Middle Ages.

With its carapace, the glyptodon, or giant armadillo, did not fear any enemies except humans, who turned it over in order to stab its belly.

The prehistoric horse was a game animal before becoming domesticated, as shown in this painting in the cave at Lascaux (south-central France).

 ## Is It Possible to Re-create Extinct Species?

With appropriate crossbreeding of cattle from Camargue (southern France), from Spain, and from Corsica, scientists were able (almost) to re-create the extinct auroch. Similarly, wild horses of the past were reconstructed. Some scientists believe that one day it will be possible to revive mammoths with genetic engineering of their frozen cells and even to re-create dinosaurs by reconstructing their chromosomes. All this is certainly still very vague and seems quite far away. But who knows?

Other similar giant birds, the moas, or *Dinornis* ("terrible birds"), lived in New Zealand. They were even larger than *Aepyornis* but more slender. The most remarkable species reached 3.50 meters (12 feet). It was the tallest bird that ever lived.

When the Maoris landed on the archipelago later to be called New Zealand, moas were still alive. The Maoris hunted them for their meat, their feathers, and their eggs. To capture such birds was not easy. The Maoris attacked them with clubs. While the moa in self-defense gave them terrible blows with one of its legs, Maoris hit the other leg to make the animal fall.

Moas became extinct only in the sixteenth or seventeenth century. A small species, the size of a turkey, survived much later. It is noteworthy that moas, according to the oral traditions of the Maoris, had brilliant colors whereas mummified individuals found later had brown feathers.

Other giant birds, some of which could fly, also lived during the Quaternary: a monstrous vulture, an immense albatross, a colossal pelican, and a swan so heavy that it certainly never took off from the water.

Strange Insular Fauna

Not long ago, French scientists found in New Caledonia geologically recent fossils of really strange animals.

For instance, on that island lived a giant terrestrial bird *Sylviornis* ("first bird"). We do not yet know how to classify it. It lived together with a giant two-horned turtle, an equally huge monitor *(Varanus),* and a crocodile with primitive characteristics, as well as other bizarre birds.

On other islands, extraordinary animals also survived for very long periods, sometimes up to the last few centuries, for example, birds on the islands of Reunion, Maurice, and Rodriguez in the Indian Ocean. The most famous is the dodo, a kind of giant fat pigeon adapted to terrestrial life. They disappeared between 1680 and 1760.

But this time, contrary to the case of the dinosaurs, there is no mystery involved. Extinction of these birds is entirely due to the action of human beings. By hunting, trapping, trading of furs and skins, introduction of foreign species, and destruction of natural environments, humans succeeded in accomplishing, so to speak,

Maoris attack a moa. *Humans are responsible for the disappearance of this bird, which we know very well: the mummified remains of 140 moas that sank in a swamp were found.*

When Were They Domesticated?

Given below, in years before the birth of Christ, are the approximate dates of domestication of certain species.

Species	Date	Species	Date
Sheep	8500	Cat	2500
Goat	8500	Rooster	2500
Dog	8000	Bee	2500
Pig	7000	Donkey	2000
Cattle	6000	Duck	700
Horse	4000	Rabbit	100 SC
Goose	3000		

a few decades, what took nature thousands or millions of years: the complete extinction of a species.

The Action of Humans and of Nature

The appearance of human beings led to the extinction of a certain number of species that before could have lived undisturbed.

Perhaps prehistoric hunters were responsible for the extinction of the mammoth. During historic times, countless species have been destroyed by humans. Besides aurochs, moas, and dodos, we can mention the North Ameri-can passenger pigeon, Steller sea cow, the quagga zebra, an many others.

Nevertheless, the impo tance of human intervention i changes that took place in th Quaternary fauna should n be overstated. Unquestio ably, hunting took a heavy to of certain species. Furthe more, domestication of dog cats, sheep, cattle, horses, an poultry deeply modified the lineages.

However, for most of t fauna, only natural laws led the disappearance of certa species as well as to th appearance of new ones.

What do we know abo these laws? Have we been ab

Family tree of the animal kingdom from invertebrates to fish as established zoologists and paleontologists. Many details are still debated.

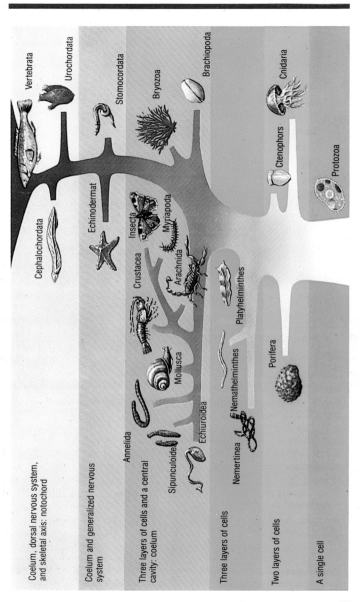

Vertebrata

Urochordata

Stomocordata

Bryozoa

Brachiopoda

Cnidaria

Cephalochordata

Echinodermat

Insecta

Myriapoda

Ctenophors

Protozoa

Crustacea

Arachnida

Platyhelminthes

Annelida

Echiuroidea

Sipunculoidea

Nemertinea

Mollusca

Nemathelminthes

Porifera

Coelum, dorsal nervous system, and skeletal axis: notochord

Coelum and generalized nervous system

Three layers of cells and a central cavity: coelum

Three layers of cells

Two layers of cells

A single cell

67

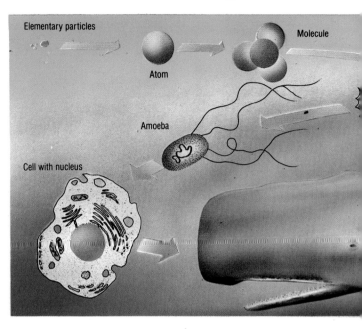

Elementary particles

Atom

Molecule

Amoeba

Cell with nucleus

to unravel the processes of this complex evolution that sometimes leads to a dead end, as for dinosaurs, but nevertheless allowed the development of increasingly organized species, among which the human species is most advanced?

Three Famous Theories: Lamarck, Darwin, and Mendel

In this book we have encountered many different forms of evolution: plants and animals evolving from seas to land, variation among living beings according to modification in the environment, changes in behavior or aspect in response to environment, and so forth. How did all these evolutionary changes happen?

The French naturalist Jean-Baptiste de Lamarck (1744 – 1829) wrote in his book *Zoological Philosophy* (published in 1809) that the study of successive organisms shows that they become more and more complex. Although he believed in some effects of changes of the environment, his major concept was that of the use or disuse of organs. He

This schematic picture shows the transition between elementary particles and a complex being (here the sperm whale) through the following stages: atom, molecule, virus, cell without nucleus (amoeba), cell with nucleus. Obviously, many cells are needed to build a sperm whale.

believed that any constantly used organ would increase in size or efficiency in successive generations so that a characteristic acquired by an individual organism during its life would be inherited by its descendants. This is the theory of the *inheritance of acquired characteristics*.

Charles Darwin (1809 – 1882), a British naturalist, wondered in his book *On The*

Origin of Species (1859) how new characteristics arise. He initially adopted Lamarck's views and also believed that species change slowly in response to changes in their environment. He observed great variation among individuals and believed that some of this variation is hereditary. According to him, most animals produce large numbers of eggs or offspring, but

Lamarck's explanation for the length of a giraffe's neck (top) has been replaced by Darwin's theory (lower). According to Darwin a long neck was a natural variation that became more common in the population because it gave a giraffe possessing it an advantage in obtaining food from tall trees, and thus a greater chance for reproductive success.

through successive generations only the better adapted individuals are able to become mature, reproduce, and hence survive. They would eventually by means of this process of *natural selection* occupy an entire environment and fewer less well adapted animals would survive. Darwin

believed in blending inheritance (like mixing paint colors, for instance) in which parental traits are equally mixed in their offspring.

Georg Johann Mendel (1822 – 1884), a Moravian monk, amateur plant breeder, and investigator of almost 30,000 pea plants, proposed the con-

What If They Had Not All Disappeared?

Humans walked in the middle of vast African swamps insensitive to the hot and moist atmosphere and bites of mosquitoes. They went toward Lake Tele (in the Democratic Republic of the Congo), where at regular intervals strange animals were reported that may have been dinosaurs!

At first, this idea seems crazy, but there are numerous records of such expeditions. Theoretically, the rediscovery of a dinosaur is no more impossible than that of the okapi or the coelacanth. This is true only in theory, however, because for a species to perpetuate itself, several individuals capable of reproduction must exist. The question may be asked how tens of dinosaurs could have remained unnoticed for so long, even in the heart of Africa.

Christmas 1938. *Thunderclap in the quiet skies of zoology: a living coelacanth has just been discovered! This primitive fish, living in the waters off the Comoro Islands, has been studied in detail over the past years. Notice its fins, which look almost like legs.*

cept of *particulate inheritance* (particulate meaning "composed of distinct particles") and of *dominant* and *recessive* (latent) traits. This concept was based on his studies of the inheritance of variations based on the repeated crossbreeding of pea plants. He observed that the seed color, green or yellow, for instance, was controlled by a pair of hereditary factors derived from the plants' parents and that the behavior of these factors followed precise rules. According to him, characters of both parents are not equally blended in their offspring, as believed by Darwin, but certain particles (not yet called genes) were responsible for the presence or absence of certain traits in successive generations.

Mendel's paper was published in 1866 in an obscure local periodical. It was rediscovered in 1900 and prompted a decades-long microscopic investigation of the cell, the nucleus, and the chromosomes—namely, the science of *cytogenetics* (study of the cell)—in order to find out where the Mendelian "particles" were and what they did in reality. Today's science of genetics is in full development and holds the explanation for the actual mechanisms of evolution.

Heredity lies in chromosomes, threadlike bodies located inside the nucleus of cells. Chromosomes consist of genes. Genes are arranged in chains on the famous double-helix molecule of DNA, the substance forming chromosomes (deoxyribonucleic acid).

The spirally shaped chains of the double helix are made of nucleotides consisting of sugar and phosphate. These chains are connected by "ladder rungs" representing four bases, guanine, adenine, thymine, and cytosine. The order of succession of these bases forms the genetic alphabet. Possible combinations represent the genetic code.

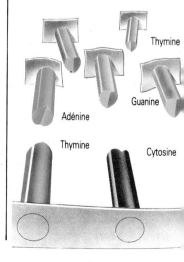

Thymine

Guanine

Adénine

Thymine

Cytosine

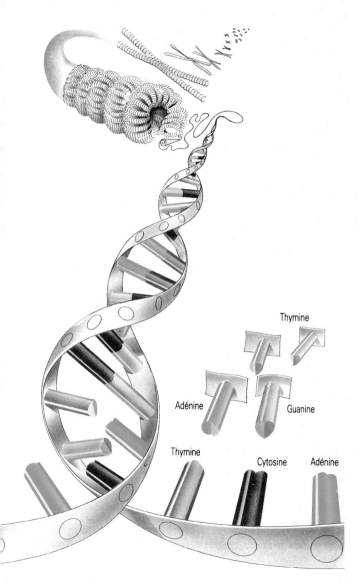

Thymine

Adénine

Guanine

Thymine

Cytosine

Adénine

73

Contribution of Genetics

Lamarck's and Darwin's views are now out-of-date. Neither knew the laws of genetics, a branch of biology that developed in the twentieth century.

It is known today that heredity lies in chromosomes, threadlike bodies located inside the nucleus of cells that form living beings. Each portion of a chromosome carries a coded message indicating how a given part of an organism should be built—the gene (hence the name genetics).

Chromosomes and genes often undergo "accidents," called mutations. As a result, the descendant of an organism that underwent such an accident will have a different look from its ancestor. Among such mutations are the bulldog, the bare-necked chicken, the red fish called the "Siamese fighting fish," the merino, and the white blackbird.

Mutations are thus responsible for variation in species. Are they sufficient to explain evolution? Neo-Darwinians say yes, if natural selection acts on them with preservation of the best adapted species.

Neo-Lamarckians believe, on the contrary, that mutations are variations that are too small and are generally harmful. They think that other factors should be considered, perhaps the influence of the environment or at least the appearance of new genes.

In short, debates on evolution remain alive.

Another difficult question is, oes evolution continue? or the time being, the only ure answers are in the realm f science fiction.

These individuals of Homo habilis, hunters and makers of primitive tools, are among our closer ancestors. They appeared in the middle of the Quaternary, about 2 million years ago. A new adventure began: Prehistoric times.

Index

Italicized numbers refer to illustrations

BARRON'S
FOCUS ON SCIENCE Series

Now young readers can feel all the excitement of scientific discovery! This series features lively texts plus lots of sparkling full-color photographs, drawings, maps, and diagrams. Each topic is clearly covered from its many angles, and all scientific concepts are thoroughly explained in simple terms. Each book is pocket size, and contains a handy index and a complete bibliography. *(Ages 13 and up)* Each book: Paperback, $4.95, Can. $6.95, 80 pp., 4¼" × 7⅛"

ISBN Prefix: 0-8120

THE ORIGIN OF LIFE
By Bernard Hagene and Charles Lenay

The many kinds of dinosaurs and other pre-civilization animals are explored here. Contains 53 full-color illustrations. (3836-3)

VOLCANOES
By Pierre Kohler

This colorful book explains what volcanoes are, how they're connected to earthquakes, and similar earth science topics. Contains 48 full-color illustrations. (3832-0)

DINOSAURS and Other Extinct Animals
By Gabriel Beaufay

This interesting book explains how our planet came into existence. Contains 58 full-color illustrations. (3841-X)

LIFE AND DEATH OF DINOSAURS
By Pascale Chenel

Here's a close-up look at how dinosaurs lived and how they became extinct. Contains 46 full-color illustrations. (3840-1)

PREHISTORY
By Jean-Jacques Barloy

The evolution of human beings is the focus of this exciting book. Contains 57 full-color illustrations. (5835-5)

All prices are in U.S. and Canadian dollars and subject to change without notice. At your bookseller, or order direct adding 10% postage (minimum charge $1.50), N.Y. residents add sales tax.

Barron's Educational Series, Inc.
250 Wireless Boulevard, Hauppauge, NY 11788
Call toll-free: 1-800-645-3476, in NY 1-800-257-5729
In Canada: 195 Allstate Parkway, Markham, Ontario L3R4T8